THINK - Cricket

Compete Mentally

by
Christopher Bazalgette
and
John Appleyard

First published in 2001

EMPIRE PUBLICATIONS LTD
1 Newton Street, Manchester M1 1HW

© 2001 Christopher Bazalgette and John Appleyard

Illustrations: Jocelyn Galsworthy and Graham Fielding
Cover: Ashley Shaw
Cover photo: Stuart Fish
Thanks to Chris Sharp and Stretford CC

ISBN   1-901-746-186

Designed and Typeset by
Mike Hubbard
and printed in Great Britain
by Cox and Wyman, Cardiff Road,
Reading, Berkshire RG1 8EX

Contents

The Thinker by kind permission of Musée Rodin, Paris

Acknowledgements

When writing a first book there is an urgency for all component parts to come together with the least delay, therefore the authors would like to express their wholehearted appreciation to everyone who has contributed to this task, because besides the contribution there was always an immediate deadline. Jocelyn Galsworthy provided inspiration as well as her very special artistry with many of the cartoons, successfully interpreting our sketches. They are enormously grateful to Robin Smith for writing his Foreword, to Christopher Laine for contributions to the chapter on wicket-keeping, to Gary Palmer for his expert advice on close-catching techniques and Graham Fielding for his cartoons.

They would like to thank the Rodin Museum in Paris for graciously permitting the reproduction of

'The Thinker'. They are indebted to David Money, the successful author and cricketer, for his contributions to the subject matter and manuscript presentation.

The authors recognise the patience and understanding of Empire Publications Ltd for showing both faith and confidence in publishing this book.

Finally they wish to thank their many cricketing friends who gave their encouragement and shared their experiences with enthusiasm.

Foreword
by Robin Smith

So many professional cricketers and administrators think about cricket throughout most of their lives.

THINK – Cricket goes very much further as this book opens the door to so many secrets that previously have been accessible to the privileged few.

Whenever the National team loses badly, one reads: "Does the team have the mental toughness?" or "Do they have the strength of character to win?" These are all mind games.

Although **THINK – Cricket** is mainly for the amateur cricketer, I believe many professionals could learn from it. Whichever part of the game you are playing, this book will give you the insight to understand that, by thinking the correct cricket thoughts, you can improve your ability.

I was fortunate to reach International level and play in sixty-two Test matches for England. The contents of **THINK – Cricket** even encouraged me to review the way I approach County captaincy and I am sure there are many cricketers at club level who will find factors that will enrich their game.

Both authors are experienced players themselves and I know them to be thinking cricketers. In this book they reveal a lot more about the game than either a player or a spectator would expect.

In fact, many readers will be surprised how mental confidence and know-how can win over playing ability alone.

Preface

The majesty of the game of cricket is that it is not just a physical activity. It is not simply a matter of how strong or tough one is, or how fast one can run, but a combination of the mental and physical strengths and abilities needed to outwit your opposition.

THINK – Cricket stresses that there is much more to the game when your mind is fully focused. It aims to open everyone's mind to a wider dimension of the game, and to provide a subtle awareness that should mean better results.

Many cricketers, even those participating every week, do so without realising how their performance can be improved dramatically.

THINK – Cricket is for amateur cricketers who lack the resources to look at videos of those who are going to oppose them, as do professional cricketers, and have no professional coach to remind them of what to look for in each game they play.

However, everything discussed in this book should be equally valuable at whatever level you are playing, but it is the amateur or club cricketer who has the most to gain.

Apart from such cricketers in the Test Match playing countries that are full members of ICC, those in the ever-increasing number of associate and affiliate member countries will benefit from reading this book.

Both authors have been associated with and have played in many countries throughout the world. They have personal experience of the immense enthusiasm to be found. There is plenty of thought-provoking advice within these chapters.

Note: Cricket is a game for women and girls as well as men and boys. The use of pronouns indicating the male gender is purely for brevity.

Scope and Organisation

Our content is divided into chapters along the lines of cricket itself: Captaincy, batting, bowling, fielding, wicket-keeping and psychology, all are presented in detail from the thinking angle.

It will be appreciated how much the Captain has to do and especially if the reader is in the 'hot seat', the importance of leadership will be fully perceived.

Once the reader has found a particular factor works, then the true value of the book will mean so much more. The batting and bowling chapters should be enjoyed particularly, there the true impact of the mental approach will be absorbed. Increasing the mental input will lead to the realisation that new levels of performance are attainable.

As the most important member of the team is the Captain, first we focus on his thinking process, his responsibilities before and after the match and, of course, his leadership on the field of play.

We emphasise that a batsman should mentally prepare for an innings; he should not just reach the crease and play the ball without thought. He should be reading the bowler, looking around the field for scoring opportunities and asking himself if a tempting gap has been left open as a trap? It is seldom there because there are not enough fielders!

We discuss the mental approach of the fast bowler, his opening spell, his body language and, when rested, his attitude to bowling again later in the innings. Following on we introduce the slow bowler with variations of guile, flight and spin all demanding concentration. The bowler has to learn how to read a batsman, search for his weakness and set a trap that causes him to self-destruct.

Fielding, whether close to the bat or in the outfield demands a lot of thought and concentration. The fielder should be thinking about how he can support the bowler and his team-mates, and he will find he is more in the game, thus considerably enriching this activity.

The wicket-keeper has to concentrate every time the ball is bowled and, besides the physical activity, cannot relax. He must observe and provide a detailed assessment of each batsman for each bowler and for his Captain whenever asked.

Each match, whether limited overs or a time game requires thought from all the participants. The more 'professional' the team the more scientific will be their approach. Pre-match preparation will include a team talk and a plan for selective attacks on the opposition, both in the field and with the bat. The Captain will explain his strategy, the team will collectively – **THINK – Cricket.**

Absorb this book and realise how much the brain can assist in gaining the best from the game. Every ball requires mental input, apply it and you will enjoy cricket so much more.

Overview of Chapters

THINK - Captaincy

The captain has a wide range of responsibilities to both his team and his club. This chapter is divided into sections describing each area specifically. As a club captain he has more duties than just leading his team during a match. These are all highlighted in this chapter. Even more important is his ability to handle people and his judgement in gaining the best from each player, thus moulding a team together.

THINK - Batting

Although cricket is a team game, batting is each individual's responsibility and each team member should learn not only how to bat but also be able to perform. This chapter will help all batsmen to learn how to improve his performance even before reaching the middle, to outwit the bowlers and score runs more easily.

Learn how to build an innings to the benefit of the team and your batting partners.

THINK - Bowling

Good bowling, whether fast, medium or slow, requires a flexible mind. The bowler has to combine with the fielders to out think the batsman. This chapter reminds the bowler to think before every ball, to study the batsman and work out how to dismiss him. The art of slow bowling will intrigue the reader, especially batsmen who think every slow bowler should be hit to the boundary almost every ball.

THINK - Fielding Positions

A set of diagrams suggesting different field settings for each style of bowling.

THINK - Fielding

There is probably more to be learnt in this chapter than any other. The reader is alerted to how he can support the bowler and help take wickets, even though he is not actually fielding the ball himself. A good fielding side can destroy the rhythm of good batsmen and the more your team improves in this department of the game, the more everyone will enjoy playing cricket.

THINK - Wicket-keeping

The wicket-keeper is a special player in every fielding side. The whole team performance in the field will revolve around him. The keeper's enthusiasm and ability should enhance the ability of the team's bowlers, should provide a spur to all the fielders and supply a continual assessment of the batsman's faults and weaknesses to both each bowler and his captain. This chapter offers the wicket-keeper details on how he can read the game and be an even greater support to his teammates.

THINK - Psychology

The very word means the study of mental processes and motives; we have only touched on this specialist subject. In a way the entire book is centred around cricket psychology and not a lot needs to be added.

The pressure of winning and losing, at every level the game is played, causes stresses and requires motivation. This chapter offers readers the opportunity to learn the basics of this highly sophisticated subject and prepares them for further study, if that is what is desired.

Gladiators!

THINK - Captaincy

This section is intended to give the reader a variety of factors that may not be found in any coaching manuals. Some of the points discussed will be of a general nature but the 'thinking' approach is the angle from which we discuss this vital subject.

To simplify this process we have sub-divided the various duties of the Captain and applied this thinking approach to each area of responsibility.

Captaincy Within The Club Structure

The Club Captain should automatically be a member of the Club's committee; he will probably report to the Club Chairman. His responsibilities are numerous and involve selection, training and coaching, player discipline, as well as maintaining an image which is respected, particularly by the younger members. His body language on and off the field will always convey a message, so that he should enthuse confidence and ability at all times.

His personality will be one reason why his fellow players elected him in the first place. He must therefore always set a good example, and be communicative and efficient. Dealing with players requires knowing them as individuals and then being positive, yet good humoured, so as not to undermine their confidence.

Developing his squad of players means letting them all know his plans. Debating attainable targets, and discussing with each individual methods of training and practice, will ensure the goal is achieved.

From time to time the Captain should arrange team meetings to talk tactics and, if possible, watch coaching videos.

Targets will not always be reached. The Captain must not become angry or frustrated, as this mood will discourage progress. No one likes to fail and provided a player makes an effort, he should be praised and encouraged. Being Captain of a club, or of any team, is an honour. It is a big job and when it works well, is a very rewarding activity.

Captaincy Before The Match

Every Captain whether playing at home or away should talk with the groundsman, it does not matter how much he thinks he knows about pitches, he should always try and discuss the state of the pitch and how the groundsman thinks it is going to play.

It is of greater importance if the groundsman is your own 'Club Man'; he should be made to feel important in his role within the Club. In most cases the Captain will learn vital factors to help his decisions throughout the game; and when playing away it is just as important to consult the man who has done the work on the pitch.

The Captain has the responsibility to ensure his team knows how to find the opposition ground and how they intend to travel. If playing at home, he will need to check that the secretary has informed the opposition how to find his ground. When playing at home his other duties include arranging meals and helpers, checking that umpires and scorers have been organised, and ensuring that everybody knows the hours of play. He should check also that the opposition dressing room is clean and all the facilities are in working order, and be ready to welcome the opposition, so that the match starts off in the right spirit. Good manners are not a sign of weakness.

Once the Captain has discussed the pitch conditions with the groundsman, he then goes out to toss up – what does he decide to do if he wins the toss? Ninety-nine times out of every hundred he should **bat**. This will be a learning curve. It is very hard to put into writing the case for asking the opposition to bat first, unless your own batting is very weak or alternatively, your bowling is weak and you have a very strong batting team. However, your groundsman may suggest otherwise if a difficult pitch is likely to improve during a game.

Team Selection

In most clubs the Captain is the person to have the final choice in the selection of the team. Much will depend on the qualities of the players he has at his disposal, but in basic terms, he should look for a good wicket-keeper, as in the field the team hinges around this position.

He will need at least five good batsmen, two fast bowlers, a spinner or slow bowler plus one

15

or two allrounders. Try and blend maturity with inexperience, flair with solidity. The job of the Captain is to mould them to perform as a team, to help each other and support each other. To succeed he must understand their individuality, but encourage them to be positive and successful. It is vital to bring each of them into the game, so they can see they have contributed to the whole team's achievement,

The Captain must remember his first responsibility is to try and win the game.

The Captain's Pre-Match Planning

Before the match he should decide on his batting order. He should work out who is going to do the bowling and be aware of the strengths and weaknesses in the field – who throws right handed and left handed, the runners and non-runners, those who will field close-in and those who prefer to field further away from the bat, as well as those who can throw from the boundary. He must also work out that, having set a certain field for one opening bowler, what happens at the end of the over when the other man is bowling. Will the key fielders be in the correct positions? For instance, it is always good, with a right-handed batsman, to have a left-handed thrower at cover point, as the ball will tend to curve from the bat to his left side. Pre-planning does not mean a Captain should only have one plan and stick rigidly to it. He obviously starts with a basic plan, but must adapt to the circumstances as the game evolves, reacting to change quietly and unobtrusively, but effectively. When setting the field he should do it with confidence.

Leadership During The Match

Batting

Every batsman is nervous before he goes out to bat, some more than others, for we **all** want to achieve. Even when making out the batting order, the Captain can inadvertently undermine the confidence of a batsman.

Obviously not everyone can be batting up the order. Instead of stating someone cannot bat well, the Captain should **be positive**. He may either explain they are going to have a bowl, or discuss that one member might be able to score faster, or that at a specific stage in the innings, it might require a more steadying influence.

Let batsmen know your plan of campaign, how many runs you want them to score and how long you intend the team to bat. Any pressures you can remove from them will improve their chances. Remind them of their strengths, if you know anything about the bowlers then tell your batsmen.

Discuss the positions in which the opposition Captain has placed his fielders. Point out the weaknesses. When a batsman is out allow him to unwind, and then perhaps discuss the opposition's bowling, so that other members of the side can benefit. If dealing with a young player, it may be a good idea to suggest that he write out what he thought of his performance (for himself); the pluses and the minuses, how he could have improved his innings and what he should practise, before he next goes out to bat. As wickets fall, keep your later batsmen advised what you want from each of them. Ensure that everyone knows the position in the order that they are batting, before **you** go out to bat.

Leadership In The Field

The job of the Captain when his side is fielding is even more important. **He must insist that all the fielders watch him at some moment after every ball is bowled.** Should he wish to make an adjustment to the fielder's position, it helps if the batsman is not aware of the change.

Except in junior cricket, the bowler should know what fielding positions he requires for his type of bowling. He knows what he wants to bowl and so together he and the Captain set the field.

The Captain should advise the bowler whether he wants to attack, or keep runs to a minimum by being on the defensive, or both, if possible.

It is important for the Captain to place himself in a position where he can observe the batsman, can speak with the bowler without too much disruption of the game, and can be close to most of the fielders during actual play. The Captain should communicate with the wicket-keeper at regular intervals, because he is in the best position to assess how well the bowler is bowling.

During play, if the bowler is not bowling well, or if a batsman is scoring more runs than is

Watch the captain!

expected, it is for the Captain to suggest a change
in the bowler's field (fielding positions). Do this
quietly in consultation with your bowler, for if you
make it too obvious it can undermine the bowler's
confidence and help the batsman.

Both the Captain and the bowler will need to
make small adjustments for each batsman. It is
very important for every Captain to know what
his bowler is trying to do; similarly it is important
for the bowler to tell him.

When setting a field the gaps are probably more important than where fielders are placed, for a gap may lure the batsman into making a false shot and possibly losing his wicket.

If your bowlers fail to break through try changing key fielders to another fielding position. Some batsmen will not notice you making the change.

It is vital the Captain communicates with his team, specifically encouraging and talking with his players.

For example… one of your players may be purely a batsman but also a good boundary fielder, and therefore away from his teammates. He might feel left out of the game, so give him an opportunity to feel part of it. Bring him closer in for a few overs, probably exchanging him for another fielder. If a fielder becomes bored, he loses concentration.

If you think a fielder is not happy with the position you have put him in, ask him if he wants to move. Alternatively, if he is a specialist in speed of movement or catching, then tell him how important it is for **him** to be fielding in that position.

A good Captain encourages and congratulates his players. It may happen that you have an older man fielding in a position where he is unable to be as quick as you wish him to be and he misses the ball you thought he could stop. Remember you put him there in the first place. Do not move him immediately, leave it to the next over. It may help him keep his confidence and try harder. If possible plan to put a younger man close to him to cover the running activity.

The Captain should also let his whole team know his policy on appealing and what their attitude should be when decisions go against them. If there is no plan it is likely to be the moment when concentration lapses and a proper chance is missed.

The Captain must be forever on his guard to make sure that fielders do not wander out of position, because runs and wickets can be lost by a single lapse of concentration. This should be checked before the bowler begins his run-up at the start of each over. It is also in the bowler's interest to make a regular check.

One of the most important parts of captaincy is choosing which bowlers are to bowl, when they should bowl and which bowlers should bowl together. A Captain's thinking should revolve round which bowlers have the most ability within the team. There are traditions concerning who opens the bowling, when changes are required and which type of bowlers should replace the earlier ones.

Usually fast bowlers open the bowling, as they require the hard new ball to gain swing and bounce. However this is not the only option, for your opposing opening batsmen normally face the fast bowlers, and it may unsettle them if you start with a slow bowler. Fast bowlers aim to achieve an early breakthrough, though sometimes the batsmen give the appearance they are struggling, yet a wicket fails to fall. The Captain has to weigh up the key moment when he must change his bowlers, and perhaps in this case the bowlers are simply playing the batsmen in. At this point the Captain might have another medium to medium-fast bowler and the natural tendency would be to introduce him at this point.

But it is much more effective to bring on a slower bowler, even for a few overs, as then the batsman must assess, a very different pace and bounce. Every time the bowling changes all the factors have to be go through his mind. Some batsman take longer than others to re-adjust. The Captain must attempt to stop the batsman getting set.

When a Captain is handling his faster bowlers, he must be aware that they tire more quickly than the other bowlers, so that to be effective they must bowl in short spells. When a wicket falls, the Captain might decide to bring his fast bowler back at the opposite end to where the wicket fell. He should be also aware that bowlers can sometimes bowl better when they work in pairs.

In any case to keep pressure on the batsman he must manipulate his bowlers and the fielders to squeeze hard enough to create the fall of a wicket.

The Captain who frequently changes his bowling may be the more successful, but if someone is bowling well don't change him just for change's sake.

Captaincy After The Match

Whatever the result of the match, the Captain's duties are still not finished. He will be responsible for the collection of match fees, unless he has delegated the job to another member of the team, which is a good idea, because other team members become used to taking on responsibilities. He must be ready to entertain the opposition Captain, ensure the bar is properly manned, look after the umpires and scorers and ensure the scoresheet has been properly completed. He must advise his opponents of their match dues and collect them.

When playing at home, he should have asked his groundsman if he wants the covers put on a specific strip for the next match.

If the Club flag was flown then this must be taken down. The sight screens may need to be moved, all such duties have to be remembered. If players are doing bar duties, the Captain must make sure that everybody takes their turn, and the players should be encouraged to entertain their opponents after the match, whatever the result.

It is a good idea for the Captain to make his own report of the match, keeping the season's reports in a file, so he can assess any theme of success or failure – and even make notes of how his decisions influenced the result!

He can record his observations on each of his players and encourage his vice-captain to do the same and compare notes.

If time allows the Captain should have a team discussion on the points that arise and discuss how they all might improve. However care must be taken **not** to over criticise, as stated previously **be positive** not **negative**.

Recognise good points, which may be stored in their memories.

It may be the Captain's responsibility after the match to prepare a write-up for the local press, although he could delegate this task to another player.

The Captain's Job

Besides the administrative activity off the field, he must be a positive person. There are so many occasions in conversation with club members at all levels where he needs to be on his guard against undermining confidence.

This factor is especially important when dealing with the youth of the club, likely to be even more vulnerable than the more hardened campaigners. Everyone needs encouragement especially when they are going through a bad patch.

Morale

In the field the Captain contributes far more by his body language than by shouting and clapping his hands and gesticulating.

The Captain of the Club is a real job, with great responsibilities; and when it all comes right it is a very rewarding activity. It is a great honour, yet should not be undertaken unless a player is prepared to make a full commitment to the task.

If you are the Captain of a team **within** the Club you have the opportunity to learn the job. You only have the responsibility for your team, yet should be just as dedicated in carrying out your tasks and looking after the welfare of your teammates. You need to learn to communicate with the Club Captain and more senior club officials, as well as with the teams below your standard.

Keep your head down

THINK - Batting

The development of batting technique will depend on each individual's experiences from an early age. Much will depend on the influences of those who trained the individual, it is very important to obtain the advice of a professional coach early in the learning curve.

For whilst guiding the youth in the styles of batting, both in attack and defence, the key is to allow natural flair to blossom, thus encouraging confidence, which leads to the ability to hit the ball.

Similarly, to fill a young head with too many thoughts and technical detail, will bore the most enthusiastic beginner.

Hence **THINK – Batting** assumes that a player already has some batting skills and wants to improve his game.

Some vital knowledge for batsmen:
- Good sight
- Hand and eye co-ordination
- Timing
- Concentration
- Patience
- Fitness
- Understanding bowling actions
- Determination

I've just remembered what I forgot to put on!

Before Going Out To Bat

Every batsman has to prepare himself mentally before going to the crease. Most cricketers have some sort of nerves, because none of us wish to fail; however, this state helps us to concentrate better and if harnessed properly brings us to a point of readiness.

Ensure you have accustomed yourself to the light and if you are not an opening batsman, you should have observed the fielding positions and found out what the bowler is trying to bowl before arriving at the crease. It is important to notice which fielders throw with their left or right hand, who are nimble, or are the quickest runners.

Other factors include whether a fielder can throw in directly from the boundary or does he struggle to throw a long way. Note those who are moving well before the bowler delivers the ball and those who only amble a few paces. Make a note of the gaps in the field and ask yourself why the gaps have been left.

Check whether a bowler changes his pace, bowling a slower or faster ball, or changes his action. Can you see any signal between the bowler and the wicket-keeper? Does the bowler use the width of the crease? Take note how much bounce the bowler is gaining from the pitch and whether it is the same at both ends.

Consider with whom you are likely to be batting and discuss your running between the wickets. Think about using 'soft hands' to hit the ball slowly towards the covers or on the leg side to steal a run. When you are preparing your innings remember the good shots you have played in past innings, because this will give you confidence. Ascertain from the Captain what his game-plan is and how you fit into the plan.

When You Reach The Crease

Initially you will only be able to concentrate on staying in, so it is a good idea to set yourself targets, such as batting for the first over, then say 15 minutes, then an hour and so on. Endeavour to rotate the strike, so the bowler has to continually react to the change of batsman, which is particularly helpful if one of you is left-handed. If a fast bowler is bowling a good length and the keeper is standing back it is sometimes a good idea to take your guard two or three feet down the pitch. This is often very upsetting to the bowler as he may not realise why you are driving him off the front foot. It will also tend to make him bowl shorter, so that you deny him the opportunity to swing the ball. If he hits your pads in this situation you are less likely to be given out lbw. Anything you can do to upset his rhythm will improve your chances of success. As your innings progresses and you start timing the ball better, plan your shots. For instance, by playing fractionally earlier or later you may be able to play to the left or right of specific fielders. Always play to your strengths. Attack where you know you can score runs, defend in the areas where you are not so strong.

As your innings becomes easier, work out how to outwit the bowler. Talk with your partner and find out whether he is equally happy facing both bowlers. Maybe you each prefer different bowlers. By planning quick singles you can arrange to play the bowler you prefer.

When your partner is out, you must look after the new batsman, helping to maintain the scoring rate while the new batsman settles down.

Opening Batsmen

The job of each opener is primarily to stay in and establish a start to the team's innings, and to see off the opening bowlers. They have to learn about the fielding side as they commence their innings, being careful to notice the playing characteristics of each fielder and reacting accordingly. The longer they are at the crease the better it is for their teammates, who may learn and build on the start that the opening batsmen have given the side. It is probably of greater importance than at any other time that the strike is rotated. Look for the singles.

As an opener there is extra pressure on you when you are chasing a target, or if the match is based on a limited number of overs. If that is the case you have to balance the need to wear the bowlers down against the need to keep the run rate going. If you become too bogged down you may have to consider hitting out, even at the risk of ending your innings, to make way for someone who can score quicker. This will be determined by the quality of those following you in the batting order, for by this time you will have got your eye in, while the new batsman will take a period of time to reach that stage.

Middle Order Batsmen

As a middle order batsman you should be a more forceful player, and as such be able to build on the base your openers have set-up.

Your thinking process will have taken place as we have already described, so your first target is to become fully acclimatised to the conditions. As soon as you find you are timing the ball properly you can accelerate the run rate. While you are getting set, you will still need to rotate the strike. If successful, no doubt the opposition will endeavour to unsettle you by changing the bowler. You become the person in control, for the new bowler has to settle into his rhythm, during which time you should be able to take command. Whoever comes out on top will be determined by whose confidence is the greater.

Keep your mind focussed on the ball

Vital Knowledge For All Batsmen

Many batsmen decide they will specialise in being aggressive, taking command and ignoring the bowler's technique. This is foolish, because if they are unaware of what the bowler is trying to do they can only depend on their eyesight and their reactions once the ball has pitched.

However, if the batsman is able to recognise a bowling action and watch both the bowler's arm and hand, he will have vital fractions of seconds to adjust his stroke. The more he knows about the bowler's technique, the more he will understand how, particularly with a slow bowler, a batsman can be lured into a trap. Only then can he ensure he avoids it.

Especially For The Young

When you are a young player and you have completed your innings, it is a good idea to write out a description of how you batted. Describe your good shots and the bad ones, make specific notes

on what was wrong. Learn from a better player
how to put things right and what you must practice
before you next play a match. How did your play
fit into your Captain's game plan?

Could you have improved on it? Look at all
aspects and make a note on what you think you
learnt from the innings.

How To Read The Bowler

On arrival at the crease take a real look at where
the fielders and wicket-keeper are standing, which
should give you an idea as to the speed of the
bowler. The set of the field should tell you which
way he is hoping the ball will move, either in the
air or off the pitch.

If he is an opening fast bowler who has a third
man and no fine leg, he is unlikely to bowl an
inswinger (the ball that swings in from the off);
alternatively, if there is a fine leg and a short leg,
the bowler will probably move it either way. Once
you have faced an over from a fast or fast medium
bowler you will have noticed whether he bowls
sideways on (outswingers), or open-chested
(usually inswingers). Final confirmation of which

way he is trying to move the ball can be assessed by how his bowling arm follows through – either across his body for the outswinger or down by his side for the inswing delivery.

If the bowler is only medium paced, similar actions may indicate off cutters and leg cutters.

If you are facing a spin bowler, your initial thoughts will be to judge how much, and which way, the ball is turning and bouncing.

A study of the field placings will help you to assess this. By observing the bowler carefully, a batsman can begin to read the delivery by the shape of the bowler's delivery position as well as by watching his hand as he releases the ball. Offspinners will normally bowl around the wicket to a right-handed batsman, but over the wicket to a left-handed batsman, whereas right-arm legspinners with their combination of leg spin, top spin and googly, usually bowl over the wicket.

Concentration and patience are key require-ments for dealing with a good slow bowler; but feel light on your feet, ready to move. Once you feel confident you can then play your shots and move down the wicket to upset the bowler's length, thus giving yourself more scoring opportunities.

All batsmen should watch the bowler carefully, in case he varies his normal style, usually by a slightly faster or slower delivery.

Take care to look around the fielding positions before the bowler starts to bowl a new over, in case the opposing Captain has quietly changed their positions. Also take note where the best fielders are positioned, do not only note the positions but also the actual players. Watch the bowler to see from where he delivers the ball, and if he suddenly goes wider, or even delivers the ball earlier in his run-up. All such deliveries are legitimate ruses to tempt you, the batsman, into making a false shot. Remember he is tying to read you, as you are trying to read him.

THINK - Bowling

Fast Bowling

The Mental Approach

The fast bowler is the power of the attack, the strike bowler that has the opportunity to take wickets before the opposing batsmen can establish their innings. As the opening bowler you are the spearhead when your team are fielding. It is your responsibility to gain the initiative over your opponent's batsmen and establish your team's position as being on the offensive, with them on the defensive.

Before you bowl the first ball, your body language, the field you set, will all send out messages to the batting side. It is vital you are accurate and aggressive (even hostile) in your first over. Alternatively if you bowl at half pace and are hit for a few runs and mention you had a heavy night the night before, you will have given the batsmen the opportunity to start on the offensive and it will be your team defending. While the opening exchanges are taking place – finding your length and accuracy, you might start with a square leg, but then after three or four balls bring the fielder up to short leg, which will send danger signals to the batsman. Your job is to create pressure that leads to taking wickets, above all accuracy counts. This builds pressure steadily, until eventually the batsman's concentration is broken – that is now your chance to breakthrough.

As much as your job is to build the pressure, it is also your responsibility to be able to strike when the batsman cracks. You have to learn to increase and relax pressure and, probably of greatest significance, be aware of these critical moments. Each batsman will have different ways to indicate he has lost patience or is worried about facing you.

Some of the more obvious symptoms are:
- Flashing at balls wide of the off stump
- Becoming frustrated mis-timing a shot
- Not being able to score quickly enough
- Declining to run, thus safely remaining at the non strikers end
- Batting out of character

This last point will only be understood through constant observation during the batsman's innings. Other points to notice are, for instance, if it is not a particularly hot day and the batsman asks for a drink of water, or he needs a change of gloves.

Another area specifically in the fast bowler's armoury is bowling short fast balls, that might hit the batsman if he misses the ball, hence testing his courage. Some batsmen fear the short rising ball and will back away.

It is not a case of continuously bowling this ball, but just occasionally, once you have planted the seed of doubt in the batsman's mind, you have, or should have, the ability to gain his wicket. If fear is in his mind, it will not be long before he makes a rash shot, as his concentration will be on evading the ball rather than selecting the right shot.

An opening batsman might have a tendency to play more off the back foot; you should note this and pitch the ball further up to him. This is in your favour, for the more you pitch the ball up the more it is likely to swing.

All we have stated up to now deals with your opening spell. Your pace, length and direction are designed to penetrate the batsman's defence, before he can settle in. The factor of your pace is another critical item. If when you are rested, there is a great difference in the speed of bowling from the next bowler the batsman may find it difficult to re-adjust to his slower pace. On being rested you need to observe and look for the batsman's weaknesses, especially how he handles slow bowling, so that when you return you might try and bowl the slower, surprise ball. While you are not bowling you must regain your strength for when you are asked to bowl again.

This could involve short sharp spells to break a stand, by taking a wicket; or to act as a stock bowler, providing a rest for one of your team-mates. This might be required if the pitch is a spinner's wicket and the team's spinner needs a rest. It may make the batsman re-adjust twice in a space of a few overs. So you must continue to concentrate, relax your muscles, keep warm, and learn as much as you can before returning to the attack.

If you are a swing bowler and find the ball is not swinging, you must remember that the ball may only swing at certain temperatures or humidity – specific climatic conditions. In consequence it is your **thinking** that takes over, so try bowling a little faster or a little slower. Other factors you should consider are your body position on delivery: how you are holding the ball and your follow through. All of which are vital for an appropriate end result… the best in these conditions.

But while you are looking for the correct end result you must be very careful that your own body language gives nothing away to the batsman, who should be watching you as carefully as you are watching him.

Aggressive attitudes in the follow through and glaring at the batsman – eyeball to eyeball, and telling him that he cannot bat are undesirable aspects of cricket. In any case you may well undo your own situation rather than his. If he regularly opens the innings he may, sadly be used to such behaviour!

In fact excessive aggression could increase his concentration and instantly improve his performance, therefore being counter productive.

However, if your delivery surprises him, or even hits him, his mental attitude may be affected by a casual remark, within his earshot, such as "It's surprising that one got through as the pitch is slow today!"

The next ball he will expect another fast delivery so try bowling a slower ball but make sure he has to play it.

Finally if you are bowling at a tail-ender and you only need to finish off the last two wickets, vary your pace and make sure the batsman has to play **every** ball. Sometimes you may give him a ball to hit for four, because all tail-end batsmen like scoring runs. The next delivery is your chance to strike as you might have lulled him into a false sense of security.

Slow Bowling

Or Ensuring Batsmen Self-Destruct

Of all the disciplines in cricket slow bowling is the most demanding and one of the most rewarding parts of the game. A slow bowler, whether a spinner or a floater of the ball, has to invest all his mental effort into working out batsmen, recognising their weaknesses and imposing a control over them which will ultimately result in the taking of their wicket.

Consider the vital requirements of slow bowling:

- Confidence
- Patience
- Accuracy – the ability to bowl a good line and length
- To be flexible and adaptable when bowling to various batsmen
- To try not to have **too** many variations
- Concentration
- Accept that batsmen will get the better of you on a specific day, but be able to return with confidence as soon as required
- Knowledge of the Laws of the game
- Respect for the umpire; irritating the umpire with excessive and ignorant appealing will not further your cause
- Good understanding with your Captain

The first point, confidence, is of paramount importance, especially when you start your spell. In order that you can have such confidence you need the support of your Captain, because it is surprising

I'm sure somebody was moving behind the bowler's arm.

how many Captains can undermine your confidence, through his own failure to judge your character. He has asked you to bowl, and even being a good cricketer, may lack the thought or intuition to give you total support. Any sign of disagreement in front of the batsman increases the batsman's confidence whilst undermining that of the bowler.

You will have been coached in the basic method of slow bowling, but there is much to learn. You will continue to learn throughout your cricketing life, because this art is enjoyable and providing you remain fit you can be a slow bowler for 40 years or more.

Learning to be **accurate** is vital; you cannot hope to be of any use to your side if you bowl one or two bad balls each over which go for runs and take the pressure off the batsman. Accuracy comes from practice, which in turn creates confidence. Until you can pitch the ball five times out of six onto a saucer sized area on a good length, there is no point in introducing the other skills of variety, flight and guile into your bowling.

If you are a spin bowler, rather than a slow swing bowler (floater), you are unlikely to open the bowling, so you will be in the field for a while before the Captain asks you to bowl. This is not time wasted, because you will be studying the performance of the pitch and of the batsman.

You will have determined the wind direction, the slopes in the outfield, which boundary is nearer and which end bounces the most. Stay calm, put all these factors into your mind and be ready when the call comes. Your Captain will be eager to have you bowling if he knows you are confident and ready to perform. All bowlers, especially slow bowlers, should know how to be able to read a batsman.

From the moment he takes his stance, notice how he holds the bat and his ability or inability to use his feet. Observe his awareness of the fielding positions you have set and the deliberate gaps to which you want him to try and hit the ball. Take note of what guard the batsman takes, it might indicate whether he is stronger on his leg side or making off-side strokes. See if he has an open or closed stance. Notice whether his top hand has the back of the hand facing towards cover point or in the arc around to your bowling position. This may indicate that he likes driving. Alternatively, if the back of the hand is facing the slips, he is more likely to be a defensive player.

Now you are bowling. You and your Captain have jointly set the fielding positions, thanks partly to your earlier observance of the batsman's techniques; start your spell by searching for the ideal length and bowl straight to make the batsman play the ball.

All batsmen feel safer if they do not have to play a shot at the early deliveries from a new bowler, so do not give him the chance of watching the ball go by. As you settle into your rhythm start to explore the possible response from the pitch and begin to offer your opponent some variety. The mental battle has begun. Tease the batsman with subtle changes of pace; vary your grip; and flight the ball, putting it above the batsman's eyeline to deceive him in the air.

You want him to be attempting to attack you. Eventually he will fail to read the flight or the spin and his error will be his downfall. Your perseverance has been rewarded with a wicket.

Pitch the ball to land on the leg side and see if his head drops to the off when he hits the ball, as he is then likely to give a catch to mid-wicket.

When you bowl outside the off stump, see if he wants to play it. Then see how far you can make him play away from his body, as the farther he goes, the more likely he is to edge it. Ascertain whether he prefers to play forward or back. **But** never bowl really short of a length. If you find the batsman attempts to superimpose his ability over yours, lead him to do all the work.

If wickets are not coming keep bowling tightly, using your stock ball. It pays as with playing-in a fish to encourage the batsman to have to be more adventurous, so that he is less likely to remain for long.

Now the new batsman has arrived, he is nervous and tentative at the start of his innings; again, bowl straight and make him play with his bat from the first ball. If the ball is turning and there is a degree of bounce you will probably pressure him by placing close fielders around his bat.

Alternatively, if you bowl floaters you can tempt him to drive early in his innings; and then it is better to let him have freedom near the bat and set your fielders further back.

After several overs test him with a few positional changes in the field and start varying your deliveries. Observe his technique. As he needs to pick up the run rate, his impatience could be his undoing and his wicket fall. Always try and draw the batsman forward and make him drive at the ball; short balls will not take wickets but will concede runs. All this is known as reading the batsman.

It has generally been thought that slow bowlers cannot contain good batsmen. However, even on a good pitch, by bowling to your well-placed field and maintaining your accuracy you will be harder to score runs off than the fast man. On really good batting surfaces all bowlers have to think defensively, because run-scoring is so much easier. The tendency today is to bowl flatter (reduce your loop), keep it tight and wait for the batsman to make the mistake.

Make sure your key fielders are in the correct positions, this is always vital, as it will add to the pressure on the batsman.

Use your brain and bowl to a good player's weakness, block off his favourite shots and entice him into hitting across the line of flight. Talk with your wicket-keeper, who may have noticed something that you have missed; make a plan together to unsettle the batsman with a different approach.

Endeavour to work out specific gaps to entice the batsman to make shots that put him at risk. For example, if you bowl the ball that leaves the bat, open a wide gap at mid-wicket and encourage him to hit across the line you are bowling, making it likely he will edge the ball. It will go higher in the air the harder he tries to hit it.

You need to work out your stock ball (the one you can bowl at will) and the line that is most likely to cause problems for the batsman.

You must be able to bowl a slower ball or a faster one, and be able to change your line by small variables, so the batsman fails to understand he is under your control.

You must learn the art of delivering the ball above the eyeline, which is especially valuable when you have a strong hitter facing you. You may have to shorten the length of your bowling for a ball; but follow it with a faster ball of good length, or a yorker.

You can learn to control the ball on any piece of ground, on the beach, or by using a ball against a wall. Mark out a variety of four-inch (10 cm) squares and pitch the ball at them, the better you become the sooner you learn the art of bowling.

You must learn to disguise your variations, such as by gripping the ball differently, slowing your arm speed, running in quicker or slower.

Think of using the width of the crease, bowling the ball from further away, or closer to the batsman. All these variations must be practised to perfection.

Although you need to be able to vary your bowling, only do it occasionally. The batsman may concentrate on every delivery, which you wish to discourage; but you want him to think he has worked you out – so lull him into a false sense of security, and then you can surprise him.

Consider small variations, such as bowling a little wider, with a slightly higher loop or slightly faster and flatter – but while doing any of these changes you must be able to remain very accurate.

Unless you are a spinner who creates lots of turn, observers will not understand how you obtain your victims, so leave them in suspense – a magician never explains how he does his tricks.

While bearing in mind what has been said it is important that you continue to liaise with your Captain. The Captain makes the final decision and he will advise as to whether runs must be restricted or whether it is worth giving some runs away in return for picking up several wickets. Sometimes one must run the risk of losing a game in order to win it, but that is the Captain's responsibility.

As you become an experienced and respected slow bowler you may find wickets harder to take. Usually this is because batsmen get to know you and your various mysterious deliveries, which means they take fewer risks against you.

To overcome this try and bowl in tandem with another good, accurate bowler so that both ends are tied up and the batsmen have to attempt to break the shackles or become runless.

Always watch your fielders; they are inclined to roam and not be where you put them, so a quick check is necessary at the beginning of each over, or after a wicket has fallen.

Slow bowling makes an elegant and attractive contribution to the wonderful game of cricket and many of its purveyors, including your authors, have spent years weaving a web of intrigue. The demands of patience and mental output are very good for the character.

Summary

Once you have established yourself as a slow bowler and developed the various techniques we have discussed, it is then time to consider certain other factors to make you the complete cricketer.

For instance, on very good pitches one has to be more patient. You might find all the playing conditions are against you.

Often at the beginning of an English season, pitches will be wet, slow and provide little bounce, making it easier for the batsman to stay in.

What are your options? You must try to bowl slower, give the ball more air and tempt the batsman into lunging at the ball on the front foot and possibly hitting the ball in the air. He could also overbalance and be stumped.

When pitches become harder and truer, then you will need to bowl a little faster. With a firmer pitch you may gain an exaggerated bounce. If this is the case, then carry on, because the more bounce you achieve the more effective you will become.

On occasions you will not bowl well. Then reduce your variations and bowl as tightly as you can, depending on your stock ball.

If you find a batsman is hitting you straight for fours make certain you put your fielders deeper to protect the boundary. If you then give the ball air and he hits you for one or more sixes, ensure he is drawn down the wicket to the pitch of the ball. You subtly reduce the length of the ball, which hides the fact that you are bowling the ball even slower. This takes real courage and confidence; but the batsman then has to put all the pace on the ball with his shot.

Try and bowl a line to one side, as it is easier to contain a batsman by having most of your fielders on a specific side of the field.

Remember when you are bowling to a big hitter who has a good eye, concentrate on bowling a full length at his feet. This restricts his hitting arc by reducing the swing of his arms.

If you are a slow bowler who entices batsmen to leave the security of their crease and take the attack to you, work out a system with your wicket-keeper to beat the batsman and have him stumped.

THINK -
Fielding Positions

Arrows on field placings refer to alternative
fielding positions.

THINK – Fielding Positions

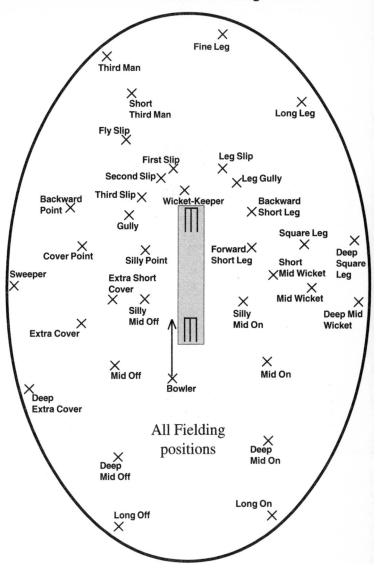

All Fielding positions

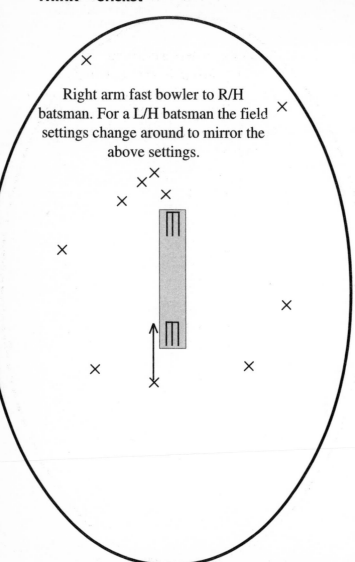

Right arm fast bowler to R/H batsman. For a L/H batsman the field settings change around to mirror the above settings.

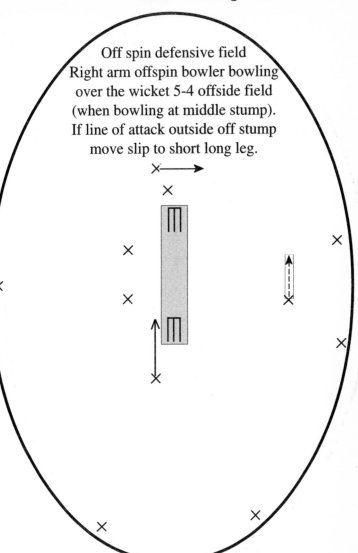

Off spin defensive field
Right arm offspin bowler bowling
over the wicket 5-4 offside field
(when bowling at middle stump).
If line of attack outside off stump
move slip to short long leg.

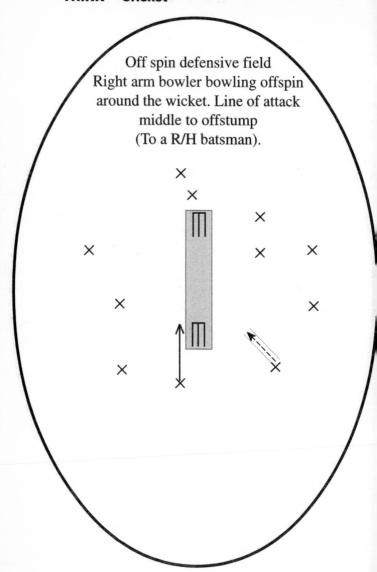

Off spin defensive field
Right arm bowler bowling offspin
around the wicket. Line of attack
middle to offstump
(To a R/H batsman).

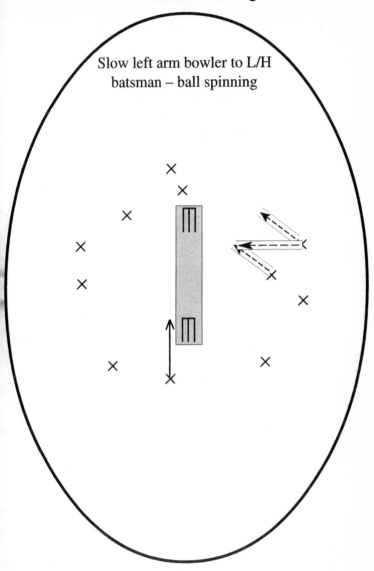

Slow left arm bowler to L/H
batsman – ball spinning

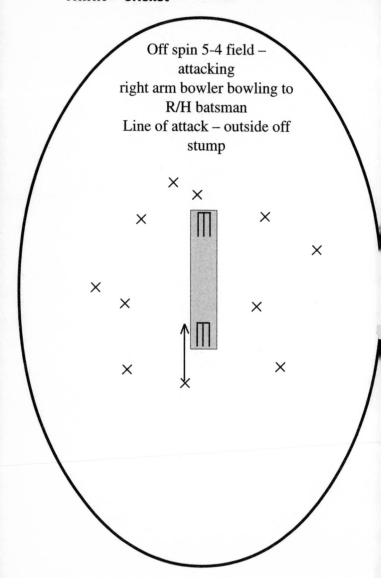

Off spin 5-4 field –
attacking
right arm bowler bowling to
R/H batsman
Line of attack – outside off
stump

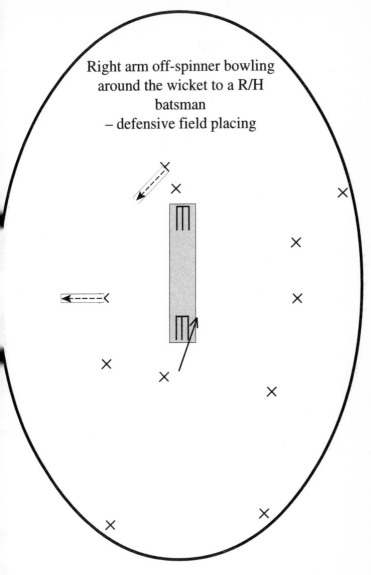

Right arm off-spinner bowling
around the wicket to a R/H
batsman
– defensive field placing

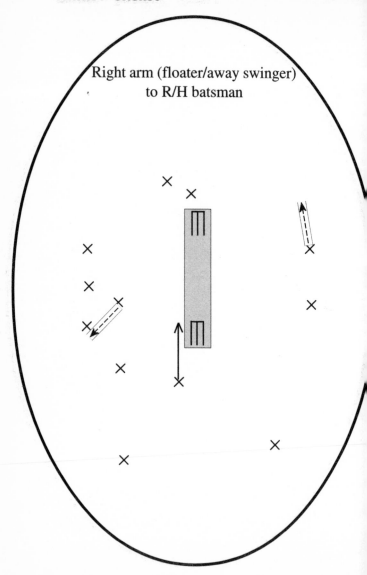

Right arm (floater/away swinger)
to R/H batsman

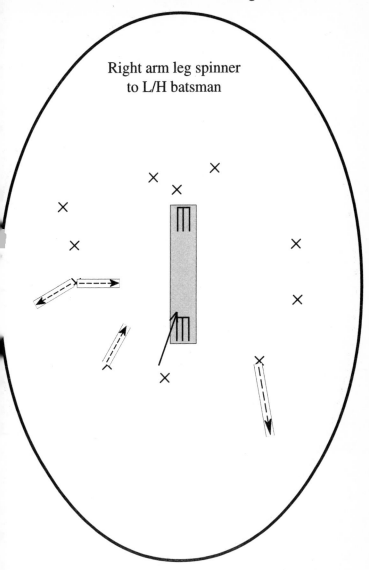

Right arm leg spinner
to L/H batsman

6-3 offside field for left arm
around the wicket. Attacking field

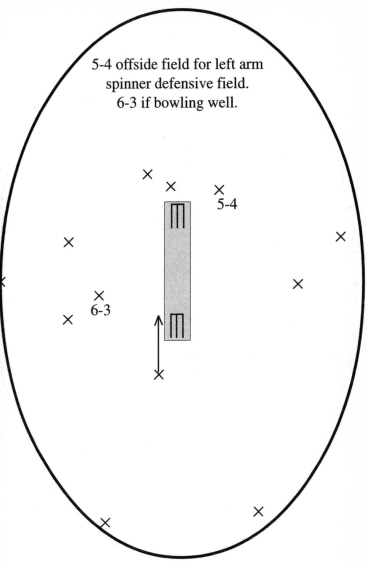

5-4 offside field for left arm
spinner defensive field.
6-3 if bowling well.

THINK – Fielding

This section is about the mental approach to the art of fielding and the various fielding positions.

Every fielding position requires the following attributes:

- Fitness
- Courage
- Good reactions
- Anticipation
- Judgement of ball speed
- Alertness
- Concentration

The more you practice the better you will become and the more adaptable you will be as a member of the team.

Just remember that you may be a batsman or you may be a bowler but **all** the members of the team are fielders.

Whichever position you field in at any time in the match you should look at the Captain between every ball that is bowled, in case he wishes to move you, this saves time and can be sometimes achieved without the batsman being aware of the change.

Fielding Close To The Bat

The slips, gully, silly point, short leg and bat/pad positions in front of the batsman all require sharp reactions. A fielder's batting experience will alert him to the likelihood of a catch, anticipation can give him more time to take a catch.

Gauging where to stand for each type of bowler will only come with experience. This will depend on the speed of the ball, whether a new ball or softer old ball, on the hardness of the pitch, and whether the batsman is attacking or defending. It

I'd rather be fielding on the boundary

will also depend on the amount of swing or turn, and the bowler's line and length. Be prepared to practice with a catching aid.

Chris Old, who was an outstanding close catcher for Yorkshire and England, says, "Close catching is a state of mind." *

All the best close catchers in the world are **relaxed in body** and **alert in mind.** If you can adopt and maintain this mental and physical state you will very rarely flinch.

Flinching causes loss of rhythm, poor movement, breakdown in technique and a tense close catcher, will drop or miss more catches than he takes. By being relaxed and alert more time may be created to execute a well-timed movement with good technique to catch the ball with soft hands.

*(G.V.Palmer, ECB Coaching Course –
Specialist Close Catching, 2001)

Fielding – Saving One Run

Cover point, extra cover, midwicket and square leg are all positions where the players need to be very mobile and quick off the mark.

The first objective is to stop the ball. A mobile, alert fielder will often deter the batsman from risking a run. Move ten to fifteen paces every time the ball is bowled, and react to the shape of the batsman's stroke (soft or hard hit).

When there is a call for a sharp single but your alertness causes the batsmen to hesitate and a shout of **no** rings out, always throw to the end opposite the **no**. There is more chance of a run out at that end. Think about it and work it out.

The fielders in these positions should always be aware which batsman is the faster runner between the wickets, who turns the faster, and who turns blind. This makes them aware as to which end they should throw to, should there be a chance of a run out. However, when fielding at cover or mid-wicket, consider throwing the ball underarm. The time saved winding up can sometimes make up for loss of power. In any case, it will make the batsman think twice about attempting such a run. In most cases it will be to the end to which the batsman who hit the ball is running, as he has further to run, rather than towards the non striker, who can back up as the bowler delivers the ball.

Backing Up

The fielders in this inner ring will be responsible for backing up these instant fielding activities and preventing overthrows. Therefore you must watch the ball all the time, even if you are not the actual fielder of the shot.

Boundary Fielding

The best runners and longest throwers will be the most likely fielders to patrol the boundaries. Again it is vital to be mobile.

Consider being a few paces in from the boundary so as to intercept the ball earlier, and possibly prevent two runs being scored. But never field where a ball over your head bounces inside the boundary.

You must be able to back track or turn round and take the ball over your shoulder, whilst **continuing to keep your eyes on the ball** the whole time – essential if you are to take a catch right on the boundary edge.

The law allows a fielder to start walking in from outside the boundary, so when the batsman hits the ball you are already on the move. Of course, you must be inside the field of play as the bowler delivers the ball.

Always use two hands to stop the ball in the outfield; a half stop often results in the ball still reaching the boundary, for you have insufficient time and space to recover from your error.

Remember that long flatter throws with one bounce will be more accurate than those thrown on the full, and reach the wicket-keeper more quickly; do not be ashamed to use this method.

Summary

Today's television coverage of cricket shows many good exhibitions of fielding. Watch and see how quick, accurate fielding saves runs and sometimes takes wickets. Enjoy your fielding and become an indispensable member of your team.

THINK -
Wicket-keeping

The Wicket-keeper is the fulcrum of every team in the field. The success of every bowler will at various times be balanced by the keeper's ability and performance. He is the hub at the centre of the game to whom most fielders will return the ball. He can make or destroy a match. Hence he has a vital role to play, his thinking and seeing role is very valuable to all bowlers as well as to his Captain. His knowledge and experience will determine the positioning of the close fielders. He, most of all, will probably be the first to read the batsman.

His first thoughts will be to gauge the atmospheric conditions, their effect on the pitch, and how much bounce each end will realise according to the bowler's speed. This will determine how far back he will stand, thus influencing the aforementioned close fielders. He must convey to his team confidence, enthusiasm and support. He has to find the best ways to do this without undermining their confidence. All these factors are part of his thought process throughout the opposition's innings. He has to **think** about his teammates, he has to concentrate and **think** about his own job, which is continuous. The role these days requires far more chat, to his slip cordon, to the bowler, to the fielders, but of greatest importance, to his Captain. Every little movement before, during and after the batsman makes a shot or even leaves the ball, should be recorded in the keeper's memory. Depending on how well he knows his bowlers, he might have to set up a system of signals or know when a fast bowler is likely to bowl a slower ball.

For the spin bowler or floater he will need to know how the bowler reacts to a batsman leaving his crease.

He has to think about where the sun is shining, as the fielders throwing from that side must understand it is better if the ball bounces before reaching him, so he can see it more easily.

The wicket-keeper is on a hiding to nothing whenever he dons the gloves, because he must assume that every ball that is bowled will finish in his hands. His thought process and reactions have to be lightning quick, from the time the ball leaves the bowler's hand, to its arrival with him, he has to instantly decide whether he takes it outside the off stump or has to go to the leg side. His brain must act in a fraction of a second, whilst also estimating any variations that might be caused if the batsman edges it. Furthermore he must assess the bounce of the ball, so that with regular concentration he will be reading its line ready perhaps to dive in front of the slips or alternatively to run twenty metres in any direction to take a skied catch.

All this requires complete concentration on every ball – the way it leaves the bowler's hand, its flight, and the exact spot on which it pitches – and yet, though alert, he **must be relaxed**, and not tense.

An experienced wicket-keeper may often be able to anticipate the movement of the ball or even sometimes guess at the batsman's stroke selection and ability to hit the ball. Some batsmen move across the line of the ball more than others, and the keeper needs to adjust his stance and his head accordingly. As previously emphasised concentration is needed to respond to all unexpected occurences within the crease.

When all this works well the keeper's performance may not even be noticed, but when it doesn't his weakness will stand out like a sore thumb.

Who would be a wicket-keeper? If he does his job well then he is a cricketer and a very valuable member of the team and he should be your first selection. If he can bat as well that is an even greater asset. If your keeper is a player who is both knowledgeable and well experienced it would seem reasonable to let him lead your appeals, though occasionally the batsman may block his view of the ball after it has pitched. It is accepted that a large part of appealing is based on reactions by the keeper, whose attitude needs to be intelligent if the team is to be taken seriously by the umpire. He should restrict his appeals to a genuine belief that the ball may have hit the wicket – and gain the umpire's respect and thus the likelihood of a favourable decision!

THINK - Psychology

To many the word alone is stress-related, and who wants further stress and mental pressure whilst playing their recreational sport? However, if you want to participate in a sport where winning and losing are integral factors of that sport, the success gained from winning and the distress felt by losing create their own pressures. By recognising stress and mental pressure one can use psychology to firstly, reduce them, and secondly, convert them into generating adrenaline. When this is achieved it is like a tonic, mentally building a platform from which further success can be launched – all sports people enjoy success, which, in turn leads to pleasure.

We want to create success in our cricket, and studying mental processes and motives between individuals and within the squad can result in team harmony, which is to everyone's benefit.

Of course organisation, practice and ability are necessary, but eliminating stress and anxiety in favour of a more single-minded approach will make the game less complicated.

The responsibility of offering this approach needs someone with judgement and sensitivity. The person might need experience to deliver an easily acceptable and uncomplicated programme. For the sake of this book we feel that clubs should consider the subject, and are suggesting a minimum basic plan. If a more specific structure is required, then professional advice should be sought.

The use of psychology when talking to a young man who has just been promoted to play for the first eleven, might follow this line:

"Welcome, congratulations on your promotion. Now you are one of this team, we have a slightly different approach to that of the second eleven. We all work for each other; we note and tell each other if errors are creeping into our play. We discuss the fielding positions and where we like to field. We try and remember the good shots we played in an innings and how we may increase these in future innings."

After the match we tell certain team members that we thought they played well, and what a good performance it was. Alternatively, when discussing how the opposition fared, we talk about their faults and mistakes.

Mental motivation must be developed during training and in practice prior to the match. It helps to set achievable targets in all the main disciplines and it is vital to ensure the team achieves them. Always reward achievement with praise, thus encouraging further improvement next time.

On the field the Captain should never publicly criticise his fellow players and never let them criticise each other, especially if a chance is missed. The best advice is to forget it as quickly as possible. The Captain has the added responsibility of not portraying his negative feelings through body language. For the bowler particularly it is hard to ignore the disappointment when a chance is missed. The bowler must toughen his mental approach and strive to create another batting error by drawing on the motivation developed by the whole team.

THINK –
Conclusion

Great emphasis has been placed on the importance that, to be a complete cricketer, whether a batsman, bowler, wicket-keeper or fielder, players should study the factors of each discipline and as such, be able to counter the thought process of his or her opposition. Even if you are not the captain, it is helpful to know how the captain thinks, as well as being aware of his responsibilities.

It is the responsibility of every cricketer, whether batting, bowling or fielding, to prepare for each match by assessing the playing conditions and the strengths and weaknesses of the opposition. A thorough study of **THINK – Cricket** will enable every cricketer to compete more positively, and gain maximum enjoyment from the game.